WRITING
FOR
UNIVERSITY

POCKET STUDY SKILLS

Series Editor: **Kate Williams**, *Oxford Brookes University, UK*

Illustrations by Sallie Godwin

For the time-pushed student, the *Pocket Study Skills* pack a lot of advice into a little book. Each guide focuses on a single crucial aspect of study giving you step-by-step guidance, handy tips and clear advice on how to approach the important areas which will continually be at the core of your studies.

Published

14 Days to Exam Success

Analyzing a Case Study

Blogs, Wikis, Podcasts and More

Brilliant Writing Tips for Students

Completing Your PhD

Doing Research

Getting Critical (2nd edn)

Planning Your Dissertation

Planning Your Essay (2nd edn)

Planning Your PhD

Posters and Presentations

Reading and Making Notes (2nd edn)

Referencing and Understanding Plagiarism

Reflective Writing

Report Writing

Science Study Skills

Studying with Dyslexia

Success in Groupwork

Time Management

Where's Your Argument?

Writing for University (2nd edn)

Pocket Study Skills

**Series Standing Order
ISBN 978-0-230-21605-1**
(outside North America only)

You can receive future titles in this series as they are published by placing a standing order. Please contact your bookseller or, in case of difficulty, write to us at the address below with your name and address, the title of the series and the ISBN quoted above.

Customer Services Department, Macmillan Distribution Ltd, Houndmills, Basingstoke, Hampshire, RG21 6XS, UK

POCKET STUDY SKILLS

Jeanne Godfrey

WRITING
FOR
UNIVERSITY

Second edition

First edition 2011
Second edition 2016

First published 2011 by
PALGRAVE

Palgrave in the UK is an imprint of Macmillan Publishers Limited, registered in England, company number 785998, of 4 Crinan Street, London, N1 9XW.

Palgrave is a global imprint of the above companies and is represented throughout the world.

Palgrave® and Macmillan® are registered trademarks in the United States, the United Kingdom, Europe and other countries.

ISBN: 978-1-137-53186-5   paperback

This book is printed on paper suitable for recycling and made from fully managed and sustained forest sources. Logging, pulping and manufacturing processes are expected to conform to the environmental regulations of the country of origin.

A catalogue record for this book is available from the British Library.

Contents

Introduction ix

1 Myths and facts about
  academic writing 1
2 What academic writing looks like 4
3 Your writing context and purpose 7
4 The five essential elements
  of writing 15
Summary 17

**Essential element 1:
Write critically** 19

5 What critical writing is 19
6 What critical writing looks like 21
7 Common errors in critical
  writing 25
Summary 30

**Essential element 2:
Use your sources effectively and
correctly** 31

8 Using their words: quotations 32
9 Using your words: paraphrase
  and source summary 40
10 Using verbs to show that you
   understand your sources 49
11 Referencing styles and
   techniques 54
12 How to avoid accidental
   plagiarism 59
Summary 64

Essential element 3:
Let your own voice shine through   65

13 Making your own voice clear   65
14 Using verbs to show your own
    position   68
15 Using 'I' and 'we'   71
16 Expressing levels of certainty
    and caution   75
Summary   78

Essential element 4:
Write for your reader   79

17 Having a clear overall structure   80
18 Having clear paragraph
    structure   84
19 Developing a clear writing style   87
20 Using words precisely   96
Summary   98

Essential element 5:
Rewrite like an expert   99

21 The process of writing and
    rewriting   99
22 Common language errors   102
23 A checklist   111
Summary   114

Final comments   115

Useful sources   117
Index   118

Introduction

University study and assessment involves a significant amount of writing, whatever your subject. Successful academic writing[1] communicates with its reader clearly and persuasively. It has high-quality content, a logical structure, a precise style and uses particular conventions to show how source material has been used. This type of writing is different from more everyday styles.

So, what does good academic writing look like and how can you make your own writing successful? This pocket study guide will answer both of these questions. *Writing for University*:

▶ gives you key words and phrases you need to use in academic writing

▶ uses real academic writing and a 'show not tell' approach to take you quickly and clearly through all the essential elements of successful academic writing:
  – how to write critically
  – how to use sources
  – how to develop and emphasise your own writing voice
  – how to build your vocabulary

[1] Writing at university is often referred to as 'academic writing'.

    – how to write clearly

    – how to edit and check your work

▶ shows you common student writing errors and how to avoid them

▶ gives you advice on the language features and writing techniques you need to write successfully.

It's important that you develop the knowledge and ability to write clearly because writing provides the opportunity for you to develop your thought processes, your understanding and your ideas, and is also an important way of communicating these things to your tutors. Regardless of how clever you are or how much you know, if you can't write it down clearly you won't get marks for it.

Writing for University shows you what your tutors will expect from your writing and how to meet these expectations. It will help you to get the best marks possible for your work and make the best use of your talents, your tutors and your time. Writing about your subject can actually be enjoyable and this pocket guide will help you feel more confident about this key aspect of academic work.

Let's start to demystify things by looking at some common misconceptions about writing at university.

1 Myths and facts about academic writing

Myth	Fact
1 Writing well is a talent you either have or don't have.	Writing well is not a natural gift but something that needs to be learnt and practised. You may struggle at first because the style and content of writing for university is new to you but you will improve steadily and may even start to enjoy it.
2 There is one standard way of writing at university.	Many aspects of writing are common across subjects and assignment types, but you do also need to develop an awareness of the more specialised characteristics of your subject, task type and tutor's approach[1] (see Chapter 3).

[1] Throughout this book I use *discipline/subject, task/assignment* and *tutor/lecturer* interchangeably.

Myth	Fact
3 You need to find out all you can on the topic or title and put it all into your assignment.	Your tutor wants to see that you can discriminate between relevant and non-relevant sources,[2] in other words that you can be selective in what you include in your assignment (see Chapters 5 and 6).
4 Writing critically is when you say what is negative or incorrect about something.	In the academic world, all knowledge, ideas and theories can be questioned, and there is rarely an absolute answer. Being critical means using this questioning process to comment on and evaluate something. Your evaluation may be negative or positive or both, or may simply highlight a different approach.
5 You should use lots of quotations.	The most highly valued way of using what you have read is to re-express and integrate it into your writing using your own words and style. You should use quotations for only a few specific reasons (see Chapters 8 and 9).
6 Being original means coming up with a totally new idea or making a new discovery.	At undergraduate level you are not expected to make a unique contribution to knowledge but to come to your own understanding of an issue. This unique understanding will arise naturally from how you decide to respond to your assignment title: your individual angle on it, which sources you select, how you use and evaluate these sources, and the conclusions you come to.

[2] A *source* is anything you get information or ideas from: books, journal articles, websites, DVDs, lectures etc.

Myth	Fact
7 You shouldn't say what you think or use 'I' in assignments.	Using 'I' to say what your evaluations and conclusions are is increasingly acceptable (but check with your tutor). Your tutor *does* want to know what you think, as long as you have formed your view through analysis and evaluation of evidence and viewpoints from other sources (see Chapter 15).
8 You don't need to explain things in your writing that your tutor already knows.	You do often need to be explicit in your writing so that your tutor can see that you have understood things. At undergraduate level, your assignments usually need to explain background information and terms in a way that an educated and intelligent non-expert reader would be able to understand.
9 Successful writing at university means writing in long sentences and using lots of long words.	Successful writing is precise, clear and to the point. This means that you do need to use more formal vocabulary but not overly complex words or sentences (see Chapters 19 and 20).
10 Successful writers think, then write, check and hand in.	Successful writers (including professional authors) make lots of mistakes and rewrite and correct their work many times before arriving at the final version (see Chapters 21–3).

Below are the first two paragraphs from an excellent second-year essay, followed by the first two entries in the essay reference list. The paragraph is annotated and has side columns that comment on key features of language, style, content and structure. Other common forms of academic writing, such as reports, also usually need the features exemplified in the extract.

What is the main reason for the increase in sales of 'organic' and health foods?

Cohesion, flow and style

Repetition of key words or similar words that help keep the paragraph on track

There is a range of perceived reasons for consumer purchase of so-called 'organic food' (grown with limited use of fertilizers and pesticides and that arrives on the shelf without additives). Positive motivational factors for buying such produce are generally assumed to be the desire for better nutrition and health, and the belief that organic food is environmentally less damaging and therefore more sustainable than synthetic or production foodstuffs

Content, conventions and use of source

First sentence gives the paragraph topic.

Clear sentence structure that is formal but not too long or complicated

Avoiding the perceived dangers of synthetic foods – pesticides, hormones and diseases such as salmonella and E-coli – is also an incentive to buy organic produce.

The evidence supports these assumptions of purchasing motives and, importantly, also indicates that there is no easily identified primary factor behind increasing sales. Two UK surveys (Avery 2006, Hallam 2003) found that the concerns of consumers who buy health foods include use of pesticides, antibiotics, food additives and fear of food-related diseases. Another study (Huber et al. 2011) found that perceived benefits to health were the most important motivational factor in buying organic produce. However, other research contradicts the findings of these three studies and suggests that health, food safety and care for the environment are not in fact strong motivational factors in consumers' intention to buy organic products (Michaelidou and Hassan 2008, Smith and Palasino 2010, cited in Cabuk et al. 2014).

The issue then, is whether we can identify any of the reasons for buying organic food outlined above as more important than others and if not, what further …

Words that make links within and between sentences

Formal words (but not overly so) that are precise and therefore powerful

Student summarises sources in their own words and groups sources together to support their own point.

Student always references sources

Student moves on to their next point

Student gives full

References

Avery A (2006) *The truth about organic foods*. Chesterfield: Henderson.

Çabuk S, Ceyda T & Levent G (2014) Understanding organic food consumption: attitude as a mediator. *International Journal of Consumer Studies* Vol. 38, Issue 4, pp. 337–345.

references at the end of assignment

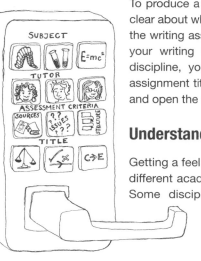

To produce a really successful piece of work you need to be clear about what is expected of you and the overall purpose of the writing assignment. The three main factors in determining your writing context and purpose are the nature of your discipline, your tutor's approach to the subject, and your assignment title. Being aware of these will help you to unlock and open the door to more successful and effective writing.

Understand what your subject wants

Getting a feel for the character of a subject is important, and different academic disciplines have different characteristics. Some disciplines, for example, put more emphasis on measurable data (quantitative evidence), while others will give more weight to interpretative, subjective evidence (qualitative evidence).

The table below gives examples of highly valued characteristics in different disciplines. You may like to use these rough guidelines to start you thinking and asking questions about what is highly valued by your tutors on your course.

Discipline	Common assignment types	Highly valued aspects and abilities
Biological science	Laboratory report	Detailed recording of methods and observations. Testable hypotheses. Completeness, thoroughness.
	Science literature review	Evaluation of relevant studies to show current controversies and changes in knowledge. Demonstration of where your study fits in.
History	Discursive essay	Awareness of the different interpretations and debates on historical events.
	Document analysis	Interpretation and evaluation of primary documents and their implications. Rigorous recording of documentation.
Sociology	Discursive essay	Development of argument via proposition or hypothesis and supporting evidence.
	Critical review of literature	Description and evaluation of the development of social scientific knowledge and theory.

Discipline	Common assignment types	Highly valued aspects and abilities
	Research report	Application of theory to real-world phenomena.
Law	Legal analysis essay	Finding relevant primary and secondary material. Clear understanding of all possible counter-arguments.
	Client letter	Application of relevant law to a specific client problem.
		Clarity and precision in advice given. Consistent use of terms, e.g. 'plaintiff'.
Psychological medicine	Written case report	Appreciation of patient's experience. Application of practical procedures to patient's situation. Personal reflection on your approach and actions.
Computing	Client software design report	Design and/or application of software to solve the client need.
Art and design	Written visual analysis	Personal and descriptive reactions supported by relevant theoretical concepts, ideas and examples.

Understand what your tutor wants

Different tutors may approach the same discipline from different directions and may also have slightly different ideas about what should go into a good piece of writing, so be proactive and ask your tutor what they consider to be most important and interesting about the subject.

The assessment criteria for each written task will give you useful clues as to what your tutor wants to see in your writing, and actually reading and thinking about the task brief and assessment criteria is time well spent. It's also important to remember that for each assignment some criteria will be more important than others, so read your course handbook and speak to your tutors to find out which criteria your tutor values most. Assessment criteria can be written in quite complicated language so again, ask your tutor if anything is unclear.

The most important thing is that your finished written piece should show that you have understood and addressed the point of the assessment and assignment title.

For more advice on assessment criteria, see Williams (2014) *Getting critical*, pp. 8–12 and Godwin (2014) *Planning your essay*, pp. 3–8 in this series.

Understand your assignment title

In order to write a successful assignment you need to understand its title fully and precisely. Your tutor wants to see that you have understood the point of the title and that you have identified underlying assumptions and issues.

> - Try to read the assignment title objectively rather than seeing what you want or expect to see.
>
> - Note that shorter titles may look simpler but can in fact be more vague and therefore more difficult to interpret than longer ones.
>
> - Give yourself plenty of time (preferably at least a week) to analyse and just think about the title before you start deciding what to research, read and write.
>
> - Discuss the assignment with other students and with your tutor if possible.

For more advice on assignment titles, see Godwin (2014) *Planning your essay* and Williams (2014) *Getting critical* in this series.

Analyse your title

1 Underline and make sure you clearly understand:

C: words related to the **content** of the topic. If anything is ambiguous, ask your tutor for clarification (you may sometimes need to make your own decision on what something means).

F: the **function**/instruction words. Does the title ask you to analyse, compare (look at similarities and differences), contrast (focus on the differences) or some of these things together? Check the meaning of the function words. If your title has the words *argue* or *discuss* in it, ask your tutor what they mean by an argument or a discussion in an assignment, as these terms can be interpreted differently across disciplines.

S: the **scope** – what you are asked to cover and not cover, e.g. specific time periods or countries. If the scope is not explicit in the title (e.g. the title just says 'people'), you will need to decide on the scope for yourself and state this in your assignment introduction.

2 Ask yourself as many questions as you can about the title:

Are any given facts accurate?
Are any cause–effect relationships implied and if so, can they be challenged?
Are there any underlying assumptions or value judgements?
Are there any hidden questions or issues?
What is the fundamental and most controversial point of the title?

Below are examples of a discursive essay and a business report assignment title, both analysed in terms of content (C), focus (F) and scope (S).

(F) Is it beneficial at all?

If it is beneficial, how much and in what ways? Try to keep the focus on how much and why it is beneficial.

(To what extent) is (global recession) (good) for (law firms)?

(C) + (S) Define global recession. Do all global recessions have the same characteristics? Don't talk about local recessions.

(C) + (S) Not corporate lawyers or private solicitors.

(C) What does 'good' mean – financially? structurally? status? Can it be good for a law firm to lose business?

(F) Stick to concise findings, not a long discussion.

(C) What should be included under 'infrastructure' - one, few or many suppliers? Where are they based? How do they interact?

Select a UK clothing company. Report on its supply chain infrastructure, its approach to ethical sourcing, and the extent and methods by which it reports its ethical sourcing practices. Make recommendations for the company's developments in this area.

(C) Should include the 'what' and 'how' of its ethical sourcing if it does any. Is there an overall strategy? How far down the supply chain does the approach go? Are there different components to the approach? Does it involve any other companies?

(C & S) You will need to define what this is. Stick to ethical, not other types of sourcing.

(C) Does it report in detail? Does it report everything it does re sourcing and if not, what doesn't it report and why?

(C) Via official reports? On its own website? Via advertising?

The five essential elements of writing

Imagine your finished piece of writing as a brightly shining star. At the centre of your star is your position on the assignment title that you have arrived at through the interactions between the five essential elements of academic writing.

The precise nature and content of each element will vary between different subjects and different writing tasks but all five should usually be present in your writing. What will emerge at the centre of your star will be your own unique understanding of and response to the assignment issue.

The rest of this book will take you through each of the essential elements of academic writing.

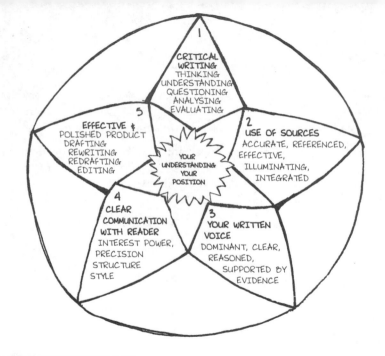

CRITICAL
WRITING
THINKING
UNDERSTANDING
QUESTIONING
ANALYSING
EVALUATING

1

5
EFFECTIVE &
POLISHED PRODUCT
DRAFTING
REWRITING
REDRAFTING
EDITING

2
USE OF SOURCES
ACCURATE, REFERENCED,
EFFECTIVE,
ILLUMINATING,
INTEGRATED

YOUR
UNDERSTANDING
YOUR
POSITION

4
CLEAR
COMMUNICATION
WITH READER
INTEREST POWER,
PRECISION
STRUCTURE
STYLE

3
YOUR WRITTEN
VOICE
DOMINANT, CLEAR,
REASONED,
SUPPORTED BY
EVIDENCE

Summary

- Tutors may differ in how they see the discipline and in what they regard as the most important assessment criteria. Be proactive and find out what your tutor feels is most important.

- Understanding your assessment criteria is important but try not to get obsessed by them – they should act as a reminder of what you are trying to do. Read your assessment regulations, as no matter how fantastic your work is, if you don't follow the submission rules and deadlines you may end up getting 0%.

- Don't make the mistake of reading your assignment title quickly, assuming you know what it means and then plunging into unfocused reading. Misunderstanding the assignment title is a common cause of low marks.

- The main purpose of any assignment is to act as a catalyst for learning, thinking and engaging with ideas and knowledge to arrive at your own understanding of your subject.

- The five essential elements of academic writing are fundamental to all assignment types.

Essential element 1: Write critically

5   What critical writing is

The fundamental purpose of any university course is to help you to develop the skill of critical thinking. The word *critical* as used in academic study does **not** mean:

- very important (e.g. to make a critical decision)
- very bad/dangerous (e.g. to be in a critical condition)
- to be negative/nasty about something (e.g. to criticise someone).

Being critical in an academic context means looking at ideas, theories and evidence with a questioning attitude rather than taking them at face value. It means analysing things in detail (breaking down and examining concepts and ideas), evaluating (finding weaknesses and strengths, connections and patterns) and from this analysis and evaluation, deciding what you think about the issue, how important or relevant you think it is and why.

At the start of your studies you may feel that it isn't right or possible to take a critical approach to the work of experts. However, you need to try and get over this feeling and accept that taking a critical approach to your subject is what you are at university to do. It is difficult work, and you will not be expected to have highly developed critical skills right from the start but to develop them over the time of your course.

Your tutors and assessment criteria will use phrases such as 'analyse the material and its implications', 'evaluate and synthesise', 'critically reflect', and 'show insight and independent thought'. These are all different stages in taking a critical approach.

For more advice on critical thinking, see Williams (2014) *Getting critical* in this series.

One common reason for low marks in student writing is having too much non-critical content (background information, description and explanation) and not enough criticality, particularly detailed analysis and evaluation. Below are some extracts from a student essay on ageism (prejudice or discrimination on the grounds of age) that show you examples of non-critical and critical writing.

Non-critical writing

Description

Descriptive writing gives the 'what' of something but does not give reasons, does not evaluate and does not try to persuade the reader of anything.

Example:

> The causes of ageism were first suggested by Butler (1969); a lack of understanding of older people, combined with fears about becoming old and a consequent desire for distance from old people.

Explanation

This can look like critical writing because it gives the 'why' and 'how' of something and perhaps a conclusion; however, explanation is still just stating fact. An explanation does not evaluate, argue or try to persuade.

Example:

Ageism often occurs because people develop unconscious negative associations with old age, thereby strengthening conscious negative attitudes and behaviours towards old people.

Critical writing

Analysis

You will do much of your analysing in your head before you put it down in your writing. Analysing involves taking apart a statement, concept or argument in order to examine and define it in detail.

Example:

In their model of causes of ageism, Perdue and Gurtman (1990) emphasise the role of negative mental associations. However, associations are not the same thing as actual negative behaviour towards old people.

Evaluation

This involves weighing up the evidence and/or argument, and deciding on its validity, value, relevance and implications.

Example:

> A weakness in Perdue and Gurtman's argument is the claim that negative associations are unconsciously learnt at an early age, because this has not in fact been proven. Nevertheless, the phenomenon of negative association is important because …

Argument

An argument is the sequence of initial claim (also called a 'proposition'), supporting reasons and conclusion. The function of an argument is to try and persuade an audience of the validity of the proposition, and usually takes the whole piece of writing to develop. Below are just the concluding sentences of an argument.

Example:

> Although the extent of unconscious negative associations with older people can be debated, the evidence discussed here shows that they do exist. These associations are harder to address and redress than conscious prejudice and this makes them a disproportionally damaging aspect of ageism in our society.

A note on thinking and writing

Thinking and writing go hand in hand, and by writing you are developing and forming your thoughts. All forms of writing, including scribbles, notes, written reflections, rough summaries and rough drafts, are an essential part of the thinking process. Incorrect or lack of analysis and evaluation in a piece of writing often reflects a lack of time (especially thinking time) spent on the task.

Below are examples of common errors made when developing an argument, with comments given after each set of examples.

1 Unsupported opinion

I have shown that there are valid arguments both for and against stem cell research and I think that such research is vital.

I don't agree that ID cards will reduce identity theft.

Problem Agreement, disagreement and opinion given without supporting evidence are not adequate as critical evaluations. Unsupported views are not usually acceptable in academic work.

Solution Evidence and examples should be used to give an informed view. If the evidence doesn't support the opinion, then the opinion is probably wrong. If the facts do support the opinion, this evidence should be used to support it.

2 Conclusion given before the evidence or argument

Ethical behaviour is not compatible with successful business practice. This essay will look at the reasons why businesses …

Problem The answer is assumed before the evidence has been presented, analysed and evaluated.

Solution The evidence should be used to decide whether ethics and business are compatible. Even if the student has reached an evidenced position before they start writing and so knows what their supported viewpoint is, it is better to lead the reader to this via evidence and evaluation rather than starting the essay or report by giving the 'answer'.

3 Opinion that is then presented as fact

Animal testing is thought by some to be necessary. This essay will argue that even though such testing is currently needed, we should put more effort into finding alternative methods for testing new drugs.

Problem The first sentence states that some people *think* animal testing is needed, not that it is actually needed, but the second sentence has turned this opinion into fact.

Solution The second sentence should say something like *This essay will argue that even though such testing is perhaps needed ...* . Alternatively, evidence for need could first be presented and from this evidence the necessity could be claimed as fact.

4 Empty, circular argument

The government should instigate an 'opt out' system of organ donation. This will ensure that a person's organs are automatically available for donation unless they have specified otherwise. Therefore, this legislation should be introduced as soon as possible.

Problem There is no real reasoning power as the second sentence merely elaborates the first and the last sentence just repeats the first.

Solution The second sentence should explain *why* automatic donation is a good thing.

5 Assumption of a causal correlation or connection

Children who play violent computer games commit more violent acts; therefore, the violence portrayed in computer games causes violent behaviour in children.

Problem A cause and effect link is assumed rather than proven. Other causes of increased violence that coincide with playing computer games could be, for example, lack of physical activity.

Solution Evidence of other possible causes should be sought and/ or considered and possible causal correlations should be described as such rather than stated as fact.

6 Steps in reasoning that do not follow logically (non sequiturs)

Identity theft is increasing, therefore the government should introduce identity cards.

Problem There is no explanation or evidence given of how or whether the introduction of identity cards would reduce identity theft.

Solution Evidence and explanation of how identity cards would reduce the incidence of identity theft should be presented before the conclusion is given.

7 'Empty persuaders' and subjective language

Euthanasia is clearly terrible because it involves killing people.

Problem The word *clearly* is used here to suggest the existence of evidence without actually giving any. *Terrible* is a subjective term and is meaningless without definition in this context.

Solution Words or phrases such as *there can be little doubt*, *obviously* and *surely* should not be used, as they do not in themselves prove anything. *Clearly* should only be used if accompanied by evidence. Subjective terms, such as *immoral*, *horrible*, *outrageous*, *wonderful*, should be avoided.

8 Statements that do not analyse in enough detail

The growth in international trade requires improved legislation to control worldwide monopolies.

Problem The statement lumps all types of international trade together and so indicates a lack of detailed analysis.

Solution More detailed analysis and distinctions should be given, for example between intra-industry, inter-industry, intra-firm and inter-firm trade.

9 Overgeneralisation or vague statements

Portable technology is used by everyone nowadays.
Men are stronger than women.
Some people think that euthanasia should be legal but the politicians disagree.

Problem These statements are 'all or nothing' or are too vague (which people and which politicians?) and so are highly unlikely to be correct.

Solution A specific context should be given and the statement should be evidenced and modified to reflect the more complex reality, e.g. *the majority of/ most/many/some/a minority of*.

Summary

- Taking a critical approach involves analysing, questioning and evaluating in order to reach a reasoned and evidenced position.

- Conducting a thorough analysis of concepts, models and ideas can be hard work and is the most often neglected stage of a critical approach. Weak or absent analysis will lead to weak or incorrect evaluation and conclusion.

- Thinking and writing critically is not a natural process and can be hard work – if your brain hurts a bit you're doing it right.

- Thinking and writing should go hand in hand as you produce a piece of work – think, plan, think, write and think, rewrite, think …

- The difference between an average assignment and an excellent one is the quality of the critical analysis, use of evidence and evaluation, and the logic and clarity of the connections made between these and the student's own ideas.

Essential element 2: Use your sources effectively and correctly

There are two ways of using source information in your writing:

1 using the *exact words* of the source = quotation
2 putting the source information/ideas into *your own words* = paraphrase and summary.

Whenever you are about to use a source, ask yourself:

▶ Why do I want to use this source?
▶ How does it relate to the assignment title?
▶ How does it relate to my argument?
▶ Have I analysed and evaluated it?
▶ What am I going to say about it?

Quotations are exact phrases or sentences taken from source material. Here is an example of a short quotation a student has integrated into their essay about business ethics:

> A second, even stronger argument for the view that businesses should be ethical is that 'good ethics is synonymous with good management' (Collins 1994 p. 2).

Only use quotations for special occasions

Only quote if you feel that you have found a powerful or unique phrase, or if you need to give the reader the original wording before you go on to discuss it. The number of quotations you use will vary according to your discipline and assignment type – you might use quite a few in a literature essay but none for a laboratory report. As a general rule, only use short quotations once or twice a page at most.

Good uses for quotations:

☑ to state a fact or idea that the author has expressed in a unique and powerful way

☑ to establish or summarise an author's argument or position

☑ to provide an interesting or important start or end to your assignment

☑ to give the reader an original extract that you then discuss.

Don't use quotations just because:

☒ you think that putting them in will impress your tutor

☒ you haven't given enough time to reading and making notes and so just cut and paste text into your assignment rather than trying to re-express the material in your own words.

Using a quotation: important points

1 Introduce it correctly

To introduce a quotation, either use the author's family name as the subject of your sentence and therefore without brackets, or keep the author's name out of your sentence and put it in brackets after the quotation.

Example:

Benjamin (1970 p. 41) argues that 'no translation would be possible if in its ultimate essence it strove for likeness of the original'.

or

> The translator should not attempt to copy the original exactly because 'no translation would be possible if in its ultimate essence it strove for likeness of the original' (Benjamin 1970 p. 41).

2 Use the correct punctuation

Use a colon if you use an independent clause (one that could stand as a complete sentence) to introduce a quotation.

Example:

> Winterson (2005 p. 3) uses the sea as a metaphor for life: 'Shoals of babies vied for life'.

Use a comma if you use a dependent clause (one that can't stand alone) to introduce a quotation.

Examples:

> As Tomalin (2010 p. 148) states, 'Pepys was … mapping a recognizably modern world'.
> According to Brandon (2008 p. 151), 'History is a record of relationships'.

Don't use any punctuation if you integrate a quotation smoothly into the rest of your sentence.

Examples:

> Polkinghorne (2002 p. 10) describes a quantum as 'a kind of little bullet'.
> One of Oswald's most important findings is that 'joblessness is a major source of distress' (Oswald 1997 p. 1825).

3 Indicate any changes you make to the original wording

▸ The only change you are allowed to make without indication is when you change the first letter in the quotation from upper to lower case so that it integrates smoothly with the rest of your sentence. Don't change lower case letters to upper case.

▸ Be careful not to change the wording of a quotation. If the original has a spelling or grammatical mistake, keep this in and insert [sic] after the word that contains the error, to indicate that the mistake is in the original text.

▸ If you leave something out of the middle or end of a quotation, insert three spaced dots (called 'ellipsis') to show that you have done so. You don't usually need to use ellipsis at the start of the quotation if you integrate it into your own sentence. There are some usage variations so check your course style manual.

▸ If you need to add anything to the original so that the meaning of the quotation is clear to your reader, use square brackets [ ] around whatever you add.

▸ If the original section you quote already has a quotation within it, indicate this by giving the inside quotation the alternate type of quotation marks to the ones you use for your outside/main quotation.

Let's look at an example of using a quotation that demonstrates all of the above:

Source extract:

This use of percentage GDA signals on front-of-pack labelling has been promoted by some sections of the food industry as an alternative to a 'traffic-light' signposting system recommended by the Food Standards Agency (FSA).

Lobstein T, Landon J and Lincoln P (2007) *Misconceptions and misinformation: The problems with Guideline Daily Amounts* (GDAs) National Heart Forum report.

Student quotation:

Lobstein et al. (2007 p. 1) state that 'use of percentage GDA [Guideline Daily Amounts] signals … has been promoted … as an alternative to a "traffic light" signposting system'.

4 Show that it *is* a quotation

For short quotations (up to two lines) you must use quotation marks. You can use either single ' ' or double " " quotation marks but use one type consistently.

For longer quotations don't use quotation marks. Instead, use a colon and indentation.

Example:

In law, where there is no *active* termination of life, it may not be unlawful killing:

the law draws a crucial distinction between cases in which a doctor decides not to provide, or to continue to provide, for his patient treatment or care which could or might prolong his life, and those in which he decides, for example by administering a lethal drug, actively to bring his patient's life to an end.[3]

5 Check that your quotation is directly relevant to your point and always comment on it

Use your analysis and evaluation of your source to comment on your quotation, i.e. tell your reader what significance it has for your point or argument.

Extract from student essay:

> A second, even stronger argument for the view that good ethics in business do exist, is that given by prominent experts on the subject: 'good ethics is synonymous with good management' (Collins 1994 p. 2). Collins' view is borne out by examples of businesses that are successful in part because they focus on the human element of management, such as …

This sentence introduces the quotation and shows how the student is using it to support their own point.

The student is about to give concrete examples as further support for their own point that businesses can be ethical.

What went wrong here?

❌ Grosjean (1984 p. 257) believes that 'bilinguals range from being very poor to being very competent translators'.

> **The problem?** Not a special/powerful idea and so not worth quoting – the student should have used their own words.

❌ Logan (1999 p. 111) states that 'The second world war ended in 1945'.

> **The problem?** You don't usually need to quote common knowledge.

❌ The main benefit of organ transplant is that it saves lives. As stated by Smith (2005 p. 12), 'heart transplantation can save lives, but the procedure carries serious risks and complications and a high mortality rate'.

> **The problem?** The second part of the quotation contradicts the student's point.

❌ Hairshine.com conducted a survey on the product. The survey showed that '82.7% of the interviewees were satisfied with the product and 10% were not satisfied' (Marchant 2010 p. 20). Customer satisfaction should be a priority for all companies …

> **The problem?** The statistics are not special enough to quote. Another problem is that the student does not comment on or evaluate them.

❌ Using animal organs for transplantation is beneficial, as patients are not forced to wait as long for transplants. As stated by Kline (2005 p. 53), 'advances in genetic techniques mean that there is less chance of animal organs being rejected by the human immune system'.

The problem? The quotation does not relate to the student's point about reduced waiting lists.

9 Using your words: paraphrase and source summary

To paraphrase is to put someone else's speech or writing (usually just a short section) into your own words. In academic writing you are also expected to use your own words to summarise a source, and so this is also a form of paraphrasing. When paraphrasing or summarising source material, you should use not only your own words but also your own style and sentence patterns as much as possible. Re-expressing other people's work in this way is a vital part of academic work, but it is a difficult skill and takes practice to do well.

Using mainly your own words and style to restate source material enables you to:

▶ find out for yourself whether or not you really understand your material
▶ restate the information and ideas in a way that supports your own argument
▶ restate the information and ideas more clearly and simply
▶ express the information and ideas in your own style so that they fit smoothly into the rest of your writing
▶ show your tutor that you have understood the source material

> show your tutor that you understand the position of key authors on a topic and how they relate to each other, usually by summarising and comparing the sources' main points.

Paraphrasing

In your writing you will need to re-express just a single idea or a short section of text, referred to as 'paraphrasing'.

Source extract:

> The whole concept of PPP [public-private partnership] is underpinned by a government desire to resolve financial constraints in the provision of public facilities and services by calling upon private management skills to increase the efficiency, effectiveness and quality of facilities and services delivery (HM Treasury 2000).
>
> Bing L, Akintoye A, Edwards P J & Hardcastle C (2005) Critical success factors for PPP/PFI projects in the UK construction industry. *Construction Management and Economics*, 23(5), pp. 459–71.

Paraphrase:

> Bing et al. (2005) point out that over the last decade the government has assumed that private sector management increases the efficiency and reduces the cost of running public services. This idea has been the fundamental driver for creating PPPs.

Summarising

You will also often need to summarise a longer section of text or a whole article or book, again using your own words and style.

Summary of one article:

Oswald (1997) argues that economic performance does have an effect on personal happiness, but that the degree of happiness depends more on whether or not you have a job than on how much or little you earn.

Summary that brings together the position of three different sources (two books and one article):

Opponents of the concept of ethics in business include those who claim that making a profit is the only responsibility a business has to society (Freidman 1970, cited in Fisher and Lovell 2003). Wolf (2008) shares this view and Prindl and Prodham (1994) suggest that business finance is a 'value-neutral' activity that does not need to consider social consequences.

Steps for writing a good paraphrase or summary

1 Read, reread and make notes until you really understand your material and feel familiar with it.[1]

2 Reflect on the material and ask yourself what you would say if a friend asked you what it was about.

3 When you make notes from original material, start to use your own words and phrases. In your notes you should record carefully which phrases are copied down word for word (quotations), which phrases are a mix of your words and those of the source, and which phrases are all/nearly all your own words. You need to record these differences so that you don't accidentally plagiarise material when using your notes to write your assignment.

[1] For more advice on making notes, see Godfrey (2014) *Reading and making notes*, Williams (2014) *Getting critical*, pp. 30–1 and Williams (2016) *Referencing and understanding plagiarism* in this series.

4 Write your paraphrase or summary mainly from your own understanding of the material and from your notes rather than continuously looking back at the original text. For summaries, initially try to encapsulate the point of the text in just one or two sentences – you can go back and write a more detailed summary later if you need to.

5 When you have integrated your paraphrase or summary into your writing, read it through to check that it fully supports the point you are making and that this connection will be clear to your reader.

> **Attention!** Using your own words and style does not make the ideas or information contained in the source yours. You must therefore always give paraphrases and summaries a reference.

How much do you need to change the original text?

This is really the wrong question. If you follow the steps above, you shouldn't want or need to ask yourself whether you have made enough changes from the original; however, it can be a good idea to sometimes check this. Paraphrases and summaries are always assumed to consist of nearly all your own words and sentence patterns and so a 'half and half' approach (half your words and half theirs) is not acceptable.

To illustrate this point, below are three student paraphrases of a text extract. The first two paraphrases have not been properly rewritten and would count as instances of plagiarism – only the third paraphrase is acceptable. At the end of the third paraphrase is a brief list of ways in which you can use grammatical, vocabulary and structural techniques to help you re-express source information.

Source extract:

> RRI [EU report *Responsible Research and Innovation*] referring to a broad policy vision to better align science and society, not only emphasizes public engagement as an integral part of innovation trajectories but also demands that institutions of science and technology become more responsive to societal needs, issues and concerns and include these issues in decision-making processes.
>
> Krabbenborg and Mulder (2015) Upstream public engagement in nanotechnology. *Science Communication*, 37(4), pp. 452–84.

Student paraphrase 1: ✗

The order of information, sentence pattern and about half the text is unchanged (underlined).

Krabbenborg and Mulder (2015) state that the EU RRI report referring to a broad policy vision to better align science and society, emphasizes not just public engagement as part of innovation but also asks that institutions that deal with technology and science respond more to societal needs, issues and concerns and include these when making decisions.

Student paraphrase 2: ✗

Krabbenborg and Mulder (2015) discuss an EU report that refers to a wide vision of linking science and society. The report emphasizes not just public engagement as part of innovation but also asks that organisations that deal with technology and science respond more to society's needs, issues and concerns and include these when making decisions.

Still too many phrases from the original and this paraphrase still has exactly the same information and sentence pattern as the original text.

Student paraphrase 3: ✔

In this first sentence the student states their own point before giving the paraphrase as support.

The student uses the source to provide support for their point. The paraphrase integrates smoothly into the student's writing, and the words, order of information and sentence patterns are the student's own.

> Technology and scientific institutions have no excuse not to realise the importance of including social and political contexts when making policy and strategy decisions. Krabbenborg and Mulder (2015) discuss the literature that is available to guide organisations, such as the 2015 EU report 'Responsible Research and Innovation'. The authors point out that such reports also highlight the importance of public involvement in science in guiding the direction of new developments.

Tips for rewriting the original:
▶ Change/reverse the order of information
▶ Use different sentence structures
▶ Use synonyms, e.g. innovation → new developments
▶ Use different word forms, e.g. decision-making → decisions.

Other things to watch out for when paraphrasing or summarising

▶ Not giving your paraphrase or summary a reference. Although you are using your own words, the idea/information is not yours, so always reference the source.

▶ Accidently changing the meaning of the source. The way to avoid doing this is to understand your material accurately and fully.

▶ Keeping in too much detail when summarising. A short summary is often only one or two sentences, and even a detailed summary should only be up to a third the size of the original.

▶ Having too many paraphrases. Continually paraphrasing short sections from sources is almost as bad as quoting every few lines. If you find you are continuously paraphrasing, try to emphasise your argument more, summarise sources more, and show how they relate to each other and to your argument.

▶ Adding your own comments within a paraphrase or summary. You need to make clear to the reader which ideas are yours and which are not, so only add your ideas and comments either before or after paraphrasing or summarising source material.

▶ Not showing clearly where your paraphrase or summary begins and ends (see Chapter 12 pp. 59–60).

▶ Not commenting on your paraphrase or summary. Although you shouldn't put your own comments within a paraphrase or summary, you should comment on them. As with quotations, there is no point in using source material if you do not evaluate it and tell your reader how it is relevant to your own point (see Chapter 13 p. 66).

When you use or discuss other people's work in your writing you need to use appropriate verbs and phrases that convey correctly what the source is saying and doing.

Use the right verb for the job

Using the wrong reporting verb will mean that you misrepresent the source. For example,

Lawton (2009) *describes* the different uses of pain relieving drugs.

is very different from

Lawton (2009) *questions* the different uses of pain relieving drugs.

Using the correct reporting verb allows you to represent the source correctly and also shows your reader that you understand exactly what an author is doing in the original text.

To help you choose the right verb, ask yourself what the author is trying to do in different parts of their text: Are they explaining, describing, arguing, or doing something else? Even more importantly, what are they trying to do overall: Arguing against a different point of view? Giving recommendations? Reporting findings and discussing implications? Below is a list of common reporting verbs – make sure you understand precisely what each one means.

Common reporting verbs

argue	demonstrate	provide
address	describe	point out
assert	discuss	portray
challenge	examine	question
conduct	explain	show
conclude	highlight	state
convey	identify	suggest
claim	investigate	trace
define	list	reject
deny	propose	

Use the right grammar for the verb

In the active form all reporting verbs need to use one of three structures.

Structure	Example
verb + noun	Research data *challenges the assumption* that there is …
verb + that	Cote and Morgan *proposed that* job satisfaction is linked to regulating emotion.
verb + what/why/where/who/whether	Lin and Moon *show why* the public is very interested in medical stories.

Some reporting verbs (e.g. *show*) can use all three structures depending on what you are using them for, but most verbs use only one or two. Try to notice how these verbs are used and check the correct grammatical structures if you are unsure.

What went wrong here?

Below are examples of common errors made when using reporting verbs and phrases.

Sentence from student essay	Problem
According to me, the issue of global warming is …	*According* to is only used to report other authors not oneself.
Kerlinger (1969 p. 1127) quotes that '"Science" is a misused and misunderstood word'.	The verb *quote* is only used to state that one author is quoting another author. E.g. Shaw quotes Berringer (2009) to illustrate his point: 'Companies will not survive if … '
As Collins (1994 p. 2) cites 'good ethics is synonymous with good management'.	As with *quote*, *cite*[1] is only used to state that one author cites another author.
Researchers are undergoing studies about the possible effects of the drug.	*Undergo* is only used for the people or things to which the experiment or treatment is done. The sentence should be either *Researchers are conducting studies on …* or *Researchers are studying / examining / investigating …*

[1] To cite/a citation is another word for quoting or referencing a source.

Sentence from student essay	Problem
To summarise Karlov's argument, he mentions that playing chess uses a similar part of the brain as playing music.	*Mention* is only used to report a minor point and so is not the right verb for introducing a key source summary.
Lupton discusses about the portrayal of medicine and health in the media.	A common mistake that tends to annoy tutors. *Discuss, describe, define, study, examine* are **not** followed by *about, in, at* or *on*. The sentence should be *Lupton discusses the portrayal …*
This essay will argue a link between regulating emotions and job satisfaction.	Right verb but wrong grammatical structure – *argue* needs: verb + *that* + independent clause. *This essay will argue that there is a link between …*
As implied by Murtaz (2007 p. 1), 'patient care should be the primary motive for developments in the NHS'.	Murtaz's statement is explicit, something he has said openly, not just implied. The student should therefore have used a verb such as *state, argue* or *assert*.
The ideas portrayed in the report are not new.	The student meant *conveyed*, meaning 'communicated'. *Portrayed* means to represent or describe in a particular way.

All referencing styles fall into one of two categories:

1 **Author/year system:** author's surname and year of publication in the body of the assignment and a detailed list in alphabetical order of author surname at the end.

Example: (Harvard referencing style)

In your work	In your references
Collins (1994 p. 2) states that 'good ethics is synonymous with good management'.	Collins J W (1994) Is business ethics an oxymoron? *Business Horizons*, 37(5), pp. 1–8.

or

2 **Numeric/footnote system:** a sequence of numbers in the body of the assignment and a numbered list of references at the end of each page or of the whole assignment.

Example: British Standard (numeric) style

In your work	In your references
Collins (1) states that managing a business well requires an ethical approach.	1. Collins, J W Is business ethics an oxymoron? *Business Horizons*, 1994, 37(5), pp. 1–8.

Your course may have its own variation of a particular referencing style, so always check this with your tutor or course handbook.

For more advice on referencing styles, see Williams (2009) *Referencing and Understanding Plagiarism* in this series.

Using referencing to emphasise different aspects of your source

1 Emphasising the information

If you want to emphasise the information in your source rather than the author, give the in-text reference at the end of the sentence in brackets (or as a number if you are using numeric referencing).

Although the law overlaps with ethics, it usually only regulates the lowest level of acceptable behaviour (Crane and Matten 2007).

2 Emphasising both the information and the author

To emphasise the information and the author equally, refer in a general way to the fact that research or other work has been done but again give the specific reference only at the end of the sentence in brackets. This technique is useful for bringing together similar research or work and for referencing several authors together.

Research has indicated that job satisfaction is linked to regulating emotion (Cote and Morgan 2002, Barrick 2002).

You can also use the passive form ('has been suggested'). Again, this emphasises both the information and the authors.

It has been suggested that violent films have a negative effect on children's behaviour (Carlton 1999, Cyprian 2001).

3 Emphasising the author

If you want to emphasise the specific author/s of the source, give the author as part of your sentence, with only the year of publication in brackets (or use a number at the end of the sentence). You can also use this method when you want to show that you have reviewed the literature and that you know who the key authors are and which of them hold similar views to each other.

Wolf (2008) shares this view and Prindl and Prodham (1994) also suggest that ...

What went wrong here?

Sentence from student essay	Problem
According to (Reynolds 2000) there is no strong evidence of long-term damage to health.	*Reynolds* is part of the sentence so should not be in brackets.
According to Padash 2000 there is no strong evidence of long-term damage to health.	*2000* should be in brackets.
George Marchais (1984) discusses three main factors.	Don't use the author's first name, just their family name.
A strong economy relies on moderate taxation methods (Sloman, *Economics* 3rd edn).	Don't include details such as the title or edition within your assignment, save these for the bibliography or 'references' section.
Smoking and related illnesses cause over 500,000 deaths annually in the UK.	This sentence needs a reference.

The difference between a reference list and a bibliography

A list of references contains only those sources you have actually referenced in your assignment, whereas a bibliography is a list of all sources you have used, including those you have read but not cited in your writing. If you are using a numeric referencing system, you will need a list of references arranged in the order you have used them in your writing, and also a bibliography that lists all sources alphabetically by author surname. Check your course style manual and be aware that the terms 'List of references' and 'Bibliography' are sometimes used interchangeably.

Below is a nine-point summary of what to remember and what to do in order to avoid plagiarising accidently in your writing.

1 No reference = all you

Any sentence that does not have any reference is assumed to be all your own ideas, words and style; therefore an unreferenced paraphrase or summary of sources is plagiarism.

2 It's all or nothing when paraphrasing sources

When paraphrasing or summarising a source, you must either change just about everything (except key terms) or change nothing and use it as a quotation – a 'half and half' approach is not acceptable in academic work.

3 Putting a source into your own words is good but not giving it a reference is bad

You should paraphrase and summarise rather than quote but the information in your paraphrase still comes from someone else, so reference it.

4 One reference is often not enough

Putting one reference at the end of a paragraph that is a mix of you and sources is not enough; you must make clear where every switch between you and sources occurs. This means that nearly all your sentences that paraphrase or summarise source material will need either a reference or a reference reminder phrase.

Example:

first/main reference

Dickinson (2009) argues that the language translation industry, for example translation brochures and websites, is the key to helping Britain recover from recession. He also goes on to stress the importance of hiring professional translators.

Reference reminder phrase

5 Reference but no quotation marks = paraphrase or summary

Phrases or sentences with a reference but no quotation marks/indentation are assumed to be re-expressions of source material in your own words and style. Therefore a quotation without quotation marks/indentation, even when referenced, constitutes plagiarism because you are giving the impression of using your own words and style when in fact they are someone else's.

6 An assignment that has too much paraphrase or quotation is a form of plagiarism

You can't really claim that you wrote an assignment if 80% of it is quotation, paraphrase or summary of other people's work.

7 Reference online material in your assignment

Material from any type of website (including Wikipedia) needs to be referenced in the body of your assignment in the same way as other types of sources.

8 Don't give the impression that you have read something when you haven't

If you read something by author X in which they mention author Y, make clear in your reference that you found the information in author X's material by using the phrase *cited in*.

In the example below the student makes it clear that he has read Fisher and Lovell, not Freidman:

Opponents of the concept of ethics in business include those who claim that making a profit is the only responsibility a business has to society (Freidman 1970, cited in Fisher and Lovell 2003).

9 A list of references at the end is not enough

Having a list of references and/or bibliography at the end of your assignment but inadequate or no referencing within the assignment itself still constitutes plagiarism – how can the reader tell which ideas in the assignment are yours and which are someone else's? You must reference both in the body of your assignment each time you use a source and then again in your list of references and/or bibliography.

For more advice on using sources and referencing, see Godfrey (2013) *How to use your reading in your essays* and Williams (2009) *Referencing and understanding plagiarism*.

Summary

- Being able to use your sources accurately and effectively starts at the reading and note-making stage.
- Be clear about why you want to use a source.
- Use a source to support a point you make, not as a substitute for making one.
- Use your own words to give powerful comparisons and summaries of sources.
- Save quotations for special occasions.
- Avoid accidental plagiarism by remembering the referencing rules and keeping a careful track of where you got your information from.
- You will only get credit for your ideas if your tutor can distinguish them clearly from those of your sources, so use referencing and reference reminder phrases to make this distinction clear.

Essential element 3: Let your own voice shine through

13   Making your own voice clear

The voice your tutor most wants to see in your assignment is yours; they want to know what you consider to be important and why. Your written voice will emerge through:

- your unique selection, interpretation and use of source material[1]
- the soundness, clarity and structure of your argument (see Chapters 5–7 and 17–18)
- the clarity of the referencing you use to show which ideas are yours and which aren't (see Chapters 8–12)

[1] See Godfrey 2014 *Reading and making notes* in this series.

▸ showing how your sources support your own points and how you evaluate this source material. The next few chapters will take you through the essential elements of doing this successfully.

Showing your sources support your point

A common reason for low marks is not making clear links between the ideas from your sources and your own position. Below are two versions of an essay extract. In version A, the student cites Baber but does not evaluate this source or link it to their own ideas – they just assume that the reader will know why they have put it in and so go straight on to their next source. In version B, the student comments on how Baber's findings are relevant to their own argument and why they are citing Bulmer and Patel.

Version A ✗	Version B ✓
Baber (2006) demonstrates that corporations using portable devices should ensure their administrators have a background in computer and network security. Both Bulmer (2007) and Patel (2009) demonstrate that staff training programmes …	Baber (2006) demonstrates that corporations using portable devices should ensure that their system administrators have a background in computer and network security. <u>I would argue that although this is crucial, it is probably just as important to have a programme of *ongoing* staff training as part of an organised educational approach. Indeed, studies conducted by</u> both Bulmer (2007) and Patel (2009) show that staff training programmes …

An example of student written voice

Below is version B of the extract again, annotated this time to show you how the student has let their written voice shine through. Chapters 14–16 will show you how to use the aspects of language highlighted.

Baber (2006) demonstrates that corporations using portable devices should ensure that their system administrators have a background in computer and network security.

> Positive evaluative verb to report Baber.

> Good choice of a main expert source and correct and concise summary of what they say.
> Clear indication of how Baber is relevant to student's argument.

I would argue that although this is crucial, it is probably just as important to have a programme of *ongoing* staff training as part of an organised educational approach.

> Clearly shows student's evaluation and own position.

> Shows a high degree of certainty (but not absolute)

Indeed, studies conducted by both Bulmer (2007) and Patel (2009) show that staff training programmes …

> Shows that student understands how other key sources relate to their point.

Using reporting verbs to show what you think about a source

In Chapter 10 we looked at using verbs to show that you understand what a source author is doing in their text. Another important and powerful use for reporting verbs is to show your evaluation of the source and *your* position in relation to source material.

Read the sentence below from an article by Deborah Lupton (1998):

> Research would certainly suggest that the lay public has a strong interest in health and medical issues in the media.

If you shared Lupton's view and wanted to indicate this in your assignment, you would use a 'positive' verb such as *show* to introduce what she says and then go on to agree with her:

> Lupton (1998) *shows that* people are very interested in stories and news about medical and health matters. Indeed, some of the most popular current TV shows are hospital dramas.

However, if your argument was that the public does *not* have an interest in health and medicine in the media, you would need to use a more 'neutral' verb such as *assert*:

Lupton (1998) *asserts that* people are very interested in stories and news about medical and health matters. However, a large amount of media coverage given to such issues does not necessarily demonstrate that we are really interested in them.

Positive verbs	Neutral verbs
confirm	argue
convey	assert
demonstrate	assume
describe	claim
establish	conclude
find	contend
illustrate	discuss
note	examine
observe	give
point out	maintain
show	state
	suggest

Use positive verbs only if you agree with the author.

Neutral verbs leave the door open for you to then agree or disagree with the author.

Example:

> ✗ Tanen (2000) *established* that visual imprinting occurs in infancy; however, this was shown to be incorrect by later studies.

> ✔ Tanen (2000) *argued* that visual imprinting occurs in infancy; however, this was shown to be incorrect by later studies.

Other language for showing your position towards a source

Indicating a positive position	Indicating a negative position

Smith's research …
    benefits from
    considers all aspects
    correctly identifies
    examines in great detail
	Smith's research …
	    fails to consider
	    neglects the fact that
	    overlooks
	    suffers from
	    wrongly assumes

Smith's research is …
    conclusive
    important
    interesting
    reliable
    sound
    valid
	Smith's research is …
	    flawed
	    inconclusive
	    limited
	    questionable
	    unreliable
	    unsatisfactory

15 Using 'I' and 'we'

Using 'I'

Using 'I' is increasingly acceptable in academic writing as a clear way of showing your tutor your position and voice (check your course style manual). The mistake some students make is in what they use after 'I' – they fall into the trap of using it to start giving personal opinions or to write in a chatty style. Remember that with the exception of reflective writing, you have to earn the right to use 'I' to state your position by first analysing and evaluating your sources. Only after doing this can you use 'I' to give your informed and supported viewpoint.

When to use 'I'	Examples ✔
When you want to state what you will do or have done.	*I will attempt to show that …* *I will examine/argue/suggest/propose …* *I have demonstrated that …*
To evaluate a source or to state/clarify your position.	*I would suggest that these findings are important and would add that …*
When your assignment requires reflective writing.	*I think that the experiment would have been better if …*

When not to use 'I'	Examples ✗
To give a personal opinion that is not supported (or is even contradicted) by the evidence – this is not acceptable.	*I feel discouraged by the current state of the environment.* *I think that we should all work until at least 65.* *I don't like animal testing because …* *The study indicates that homeopathy is not effective but I still feel that it works.* *I believe in the power of the mind.*
To describe methodology, stages and processes where it is not important who did what. Instead, use the passive form: *The equipment was washed in saline solution*.	*I washed the equipment in saline solution.*
To give information or to state a fact. Instead just give the fact: *Dickens was born in 1812.*	*I read that Dickens was born in 1812.*

Using 'we'

Students sometimes overuse 'we' because they are trying not to use 'I' or because they are trying to be formal. There are four common uses of 'we' but only one of them is appropriate for formal writing.

When to use 'we'	Example ✔
To indicate collaborative/team work	*We each interviewed 10 students*

When not to use 'we'	Examples ✗
'We' meaning 'I' This can be ambiguous (do you mean just you or a team?) and also sounds archaic and overly formal – it's much better to use 'I'.	*We will propose in this essay that ...* *In this essay we argue that ...*
To refer to both you and the reader This use of 'we' is ambiguous (do you mean just you, you and the reader, or a team?) and sounds as if you are telling the reader what to think. Instead use: *It should be noted that ...* *Table 5 shows that ...* *The data suggest a link ...* *I suggest that the data show a link ...*	*We should note that ...* *We also need to consider the possibility of ...* *We can see from Table 5 that ...* *We can conclude from the data that there is a link ...*

When not to use 'we'	Examples ✗
To refer to society/everyone You can use 'we' to state a known fact, but it might sound presumptuous (does everybody know?). Never use *we all …* It's much better to just give the fact (*Smoking is addictive*) or to use the passive form (*The addictive nature of smoking is well established*).	*We know that smoking is addictive.* *We all know that smoking is addictive.*
'We' can also be too informal and personal. It's better to write *Large-scale deforestation causes …*	*When we cut down forests, we cause …*
'We' often goes hand in hand with an over-generalisation – not acceptable in academic writing (see p. 29).	*We should decriminalise all drugs.* *We all want to live in a fairer society.*
Spoken/presentation style phrases These types of 'we' phrases are fine for spoken presentations but they are too informal for writing.	*We will begin by …* *We are going to discuss …* *We would like to point out that …* *We shall now move on to …*

Be wary of expressing absolute certainty, as in:

> The data prove the existence of automatic ageism.
> Removing speed cameras will result in an increase in the number of road deaths.
> Children are definitely more aware politically than in previous generations.

Even though you think there is overwhelming evidence to support a proposition, someone else may think differently, and even the most eminent experts on a subject accept that they might be wrong. In academic study, all knowledge is contestable and something can only be proved to be false, not true.

Absolute
certainty

Absolute
uncertainty

You can show this contestable nature of knowledge by using 'cautious' language such as *I suggest, this might indicate, this indicates a tendency, it is probably*. Don't be fooled by textbooks that imply certainty – textbooks simplify perspectives on knowledge because their purpose is to give a basic overview of the subject. If you look at a journal article in your subject area, you will see that authors use words and phrases such as *probably* and *this might suggest* to add a degree of caution to their claim. An additional benefit of using cautious language is that it helps persuade your reader rather than sounding as if you are telling them what to think.

Below are phrases ordered according to their certainty level. Use them in your own writing to indicate how certain you are about something and to acknowledge the contestable nature of knowledge.

Verb phrases

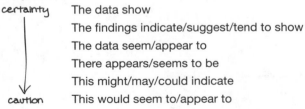

certainty   The data show

The findings indicate/suggest/tend to show

The data seem/appear to

There appears/seems to be

This might/may/could indicate

caution   This would seem to/appear to

Adverb/verb phrases

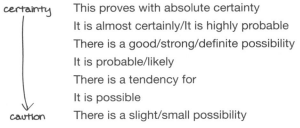

certainty

This strongly/certainly/definitely suggests

This almost certainly/definitely suggests/shows/indicates

I would strongly suggest

caution

This perhaps suggests

Adjective/noun phrases

certainty

This proves with absolute certainty

It is almost certainly/It is highly probable

There is a good/strong/definite possibility

It is probable/likely

There is a tendency for

It is possible

caution

There is a slight/small possibility

NB: Some tutors don't like the use of verbs such as *suggests* for inanimate objects (e.g. *The data suggest that …*) so check this with your tutor.

Summary

▸ The most important factor in developing a clear written voice is high-quality research and adequate time spent on thinking and developing your ideas.

▸ You need to make clear where all the different source voices in your assignment are, but yours is the one that should stand out.

▸ Ensure that your written voice stands out by clearly showing how your sources support your points and by being precise in your use of verbs both to report sources and to show your position in relation to them.

▸ Don't write like a textbook – your tutor wants to see that you appreciate the contestable nature of knowledge, so use appropriate language to express degrees of caution.

Essential element 4: Write for your reader

The outward success of any piece of work is judged by the audience, which in the case of academic assignments is your tutor. You want to avoid your reader having to struggle when marking your work because they are not sure what you mean or how one point connects to another. A successful piece of writing has good quality content, a clear structure and a direct, precise style.

17 Having a clear overall structure

You need to structure your writing clearly to allow your ideas to shine. The exact way you structure your writing will depend on your particular writing context (a lab report will have a different structure to a discursive essay); however, most written pieces will need the basic structure outlined here.

INTRODUCTION – say what you are going to do

Interpret the issue and say why is it important.

Interpret and define key terms.

Say how you will answer the issue/question and the order in which you will do so.

BODY – do what you said you would do

Start to explore the issue.

Continue to explore and develop the issue.

Push further and identify extra dimensions and distinctions within the issue.

Move on to clarify what you feel is at the heart of the position you have arrived at.

CONCLUSION – say what you have done

Bring things together by summarising what you have said and clarifying the position you have arrived at.

Importantly, the three main sections of your piece should connect logically and should match up.

Always do a detailed plan before you start writing out in full – if you don't, it's very easy to end up with an assignment that is a bundle of mismatched pieces. For example, if you were writing the essay '*Ageism is more disabling than ageing. Discuss*' and you spent most of the essay body giving evidence for how ageism is *not* a serious problem, it would then be odd to state in your conclusion that ageism is a significant problem and more disabling than natural ageing.

For more advice on essay planning and structure, see Godwin (2014) *Planning your essay* in this series.

Avoid doing this!

Use signposting language

'Structure signposts' help guide your reader through your work. Don't use lots of signposting language in an attempt to cover up a lack of good content and ideas; in fact, you can write well without using many signpost phrases. Do use signposts to make clear to your reader how your points connect, contrast and develop.

Useful signpost phrases

Saying what you are going to do/order points
In this essay I will … / This essay will …
first(ly), second(ly), third(ly) next, then

Adding another similar point
In addition / An additional x is
Another x is
Also / As well as x there is
Moreover / Furthermore / Similarly
What is more

Moving on to a contrasting point
In contrast / By contrast / Conversely

Moving on to a different point
As for / Regarding / With regard to
Moving on to / With respect to

Restating/rephrasing
In other words / That is to say
Put another way / To put it more simply

Introducing alternative views
Alternatively / A different interpretation is
A different viewpoint could be
An opposing view is / Others argue that
It could also be argued that

 WRITING FOR UNIVERSITY

Concluding
To conclude, / In conclusion,
To summarise,

Reasoning:
Cause/result
Because / Since / Therefore / Thus
So as / This means that
This results in / As a result
Consequently / The effect of this is
This suggests that

Contrasting
But / However / Yet
On the contrary / In contrast

Concession
Nevertheless / Despite x it is still
Although / However

Similarity
Similarly / Likewise / In the same way

Condition
Unless / Provided that / If / As long as

A 2,000 word assignment usually has 7–10 paragraphs. Paragraphs vary in length but as a general rule they should be at least three sentences long; if you find you have a paragraph of less than this, you probably need to either develop the idea more, provide an example or evidence, attach the idea to a related idea or paragraph, or get rid of it altogether. At the other end of the scale, avoid paragraphs that are longer than half a page – your reader needs to be able to digest what they read in smaller pieces than this.

Each paragraph should have a start, middle and end, and should focus on one idea. Each should have a logical flow and the reader should be able to see (either via a signpost phrase and/or content) how one paragraph follows on from the previous one. The precise structure of paragraphs can and should vary to some extent, depending on the writing style, assignment type and where the paragraph is in the

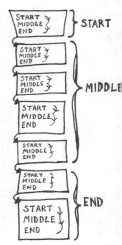

assignment; for example, not all paragraphs will use the first sentence to make the topic clear and not all will have a clear link from one to the next. Every paragraph, however, should leave the reader feeling that they have read a manageable chunk of your assignment and have reached an appropriate place to pause for thought before reading on.

Below is part of the essay extract from pages 4 and 5. This time it is annotated to highlight how the content gives the paragraph a clear structure. Look also at the same paragraph on pages 4 and 5 to remind yourself of the language, style and reference features that also help to give the paragraph coherence and flow.

The evidence supports these assumptions of purchasing motives and importantly, also indicates that there is no easily identified primary factor behind increasing sales. Two UK surveys (Avery 2006, Hallam 2003) found that the concerns of consumers who buy health foods include use of pesticides, antibiotics, food additives and fear of food-related diseases. Another study (Huber et al. 2011) found that perceived benefits to health were the most important motivational factor in buying organic produce. However, other research

Start

In the first sentence the student gives the paragraph topic.

Middle

The student summarises and synthesises evidence and examples that support their point.

contradicts the findings of these three studies and suggests that health, food safety and care for the environment are not in fact strong motivational factors in consumers' intention to buy organic products (Michaelidou and Hassan 2008, Smith and Palasino 2010, cited in Cabuk et al. 2014).

The issue then, is whether we can identify any of the reasons for buying organic food outlined above as more important than others and if not, what further . . .

End

To end this paragraph the student cites research that contrasts with that given earlier, thereby continuing to support their point. Rather than having an explicit 'end sentence' the student uses the start of the next paragraph to state what knowledge they feel arises from the data.

We have already covered many aspects that are essential for giving your writing a clear and appropriate style:

▶ using evidence and logic to argue rather than giving personal opinion (pp. 19–30)

▶ being objective and neutral (pp. 19–30)

▶ being specific (p. 29)

▶ using source material correctly and precisely (pp. 31–48)

▶ using appropriate verbs and other phrases to report and evaluate sources (pp. 49–53 and 68–70)

▶ using 'I' and 'we' appropriately (pp. 71–4)

▶ using cautious language (pp. 75–7)

▶ using content and signposting to give structure (pp. 80–6).

The rest of this chapter will take you through the other features of language necessary for a clear writing style.

Form and formality

Remember that writing is not just speech written down – students often lose marks because their writing is too much like everyday speech.

Don't
Use contractions – *it's*, *can't*, *won't*.
Use word abbreviations – *dept.*, *gov.* Use of *e.g.* and *i.e.* is acceptable when they are used within brackets and might be acceptable generally in your discipline but you should check this with your tutor.
Use vague 'run on' expressions – *etc.*, *and so on*, *and so forth*, e.g. *A healthy lifestyle means eating well, exercising and so forth.*
Use direct questions, e.g. *So, what are the main causes of global warming?* An occasional question for impact is okay but they can make your writing look informal.
Address the reader as 'you' or give them orders (unless giving written instructions), e.g. *You need to think about possible solutions*.
Use rude or emotional adjectives, e.g. *awful*, *ridiculous*, *stupid*, *pretty*, *lovely*, *terrible*, *unfair*.
Use words such as *stuff* or *thing*.
Use words such as *a bit*, *a lot of*, *plenty of*, *huge*.
Use the verb *get* or use too many two-part verbs, e.g. *cut down*, *make up*, *got worse*, *brought up*, *set up*, *look into*, *put up with*, *find out*.

Do
Write in full sentences.
Learn how to use punctuation correctly – it is crucial to meaning.
Finish your sentence with as much precision as possible, e.g. *A healthy lifestyle means eating well, exercising, a good work–life balance and a generally healthy environment.*
Use acronyms (e.g. NATO) accurately and give the full form with the acronym in brackets at the first mention.
Use the precise word, e.g. *theory, idea, action, issue, chemical.*
Find precise, formal equivalents for two-part verbs: *reduce, compensate, worsened, raised, established, investigate, tolerate, discover.*

For more advice on good writing style, see Copus (2009) *Brilliant writing tips for students* in this series.

Don't use speech-like phrases and clichés

These are informal and also often vague and/or meaningless; it's much better to explain exactly what you want to say in your own words.

Don't use ...

anyway

basically

at the end of the day

it all comes down to

the thing is

along the way

beyond a shadow of a doubt

in a nutshell

last but not least

Don't use ...

to name but a few

easier said than done

that's another story

to put it mildly

keep a lid on

leave no stone unturned

a different ball game

see the light at the end of the tunnel

Power

Academic writing is quite dense and powerful – it packs a lot of information into a small amount of text. Write powerfully by replacing subject/verb phrases and wh-phrases with adjective/noun phrases.

Version A below uses lots of subject/verb and wh-phrases. However, the reader does not need to know who is doing what, so the same information can be given in a more powerful way by using adjective/noun phrases (in italic) instead, as in Version B.

Version A – less powerful

The doctor will choose which drug to treat the patient with depending on whether they have had previous health problems and what they do for a living. If they are someone who is resistant to penicillin, the doctor will also need to do a skin test so that they can check for reactions that might cause problems.

Version B ✔ – more powerful

The treatment drug depends on the *patient's medical history* and *current occupation*. *Penicillin-resistant patients* will also need a skin test to check for potential negative reactions.

Notice also that in Version A the main points (the treatment drug and penicillin-resistant patients) get a bit lost in the middle of each sentence. In Version B, the use of noun phrases allows the main point to be given at the start of each sentence, which is much clearer for the reader.

Don't overuse abstract nouns

Although it's good to use nouns, don't overuse abstract nouns (nouns that end in *-tion*, *-ism*, *-ness*, *-nce*, *-ity*) as they can sometimes make a sentence clumsy and unclear. It may be better to use a verb/adjective form instead:

❌ The *organisation* of the compilation of the legislation was poor.

✅ The compilation of the legislation *was* poorly *organised*.

❌ The *significance* of the experiment is that it shows that the enzyme is present.

✅ The experiment is *significant* because it shows that the enzyme is present.

Don't overuse the passive voice

You will sometimes need to use the passive voice but if overused it can make sentences too complicated and weak. In these cases it is better to use the more direct active voice or change the sentence.

Passive ✗	Active ✔
It needs to be emphasised that this theory has several flaws. It has been argued in this essay that … It has been recommended by government that schools require students to …	This theory has several flaws. I have argued in this essay that … The government has recommended that schools require students …

Strike the right balance of sentence length

It's good to have some short and some longer sentences. What's most important is to think about how clear, flowing and powerful your sentences will be to your reader. Avoid sentences that have 35+ words and more than two clauses – the occasional long sentence is okay but check that it makes sense – and also avoid having a series of very short sentences.

☒ One sentence – too long

Online translation programmes work via what would seem to be the same process as a human translator, which is to read each word, but the machine does not understand the text content and does not consider the register and context, producing incomprehensible translation that is very difficult to read.

☒ Six sentences – too short

Online translation programmes work via what would seem to be the same process as a human translator. This is to read each word. A machine does not understand the text content. It also does not consider the register and context. Because a machine can't do these things it produces incomprehensible translation. This is very difficult to read.

☑ Two sentences – okay

Online translation programmes work via what would seem to be the same process as a human translator, which is to read each word. The difference is that a machine does not understand the text content and does not consider the register and context, producing incomprehensible translation that is very difficult to read.

Be succinct

Good academic writing is precise and to the point. Writing in a formal style and discussing complex ideas does *not* mean that you have to use as many 'long words' as possible, and academic articles that do so are probably poorly written. Aim to convey and explain complex ideas clearly, but avoid using words that are overly complicated:

Examples:
This essay will *commence with* ✗ / *start with* ✔
The experiment *endeavours to* ✗ / *tries to* ✔
The tower *was fabricated in* ✗ / *built in* ✔
We *utilised* ✗ / *used* ✔ three different methods

Also avoid words that merely repeat the previous one:

Examples:

absolutely essential ✗ – essential ✔
conclusive proof ✗ – proof ✔
hard evidence ✗ – evidence ✔
different varieties ✗ – varieties ✔
or, alternatively ✗ – alternatively ✔

past history ✗ – history ✔
revert back to ✗ – revert to ✔
close proximity ✗ – proximity ✔
join together ✗ – join ✔
true facts ✗ – facts ✔

Authenticity

Don't copy someone else's style or use words you don't fully understand; your tutor would rather see you explain your ideas clearly in less formal words than unclearly in complicated language. If you can't write clearly about something, it might be because you don't yet understand the issue or your source material properly or because you need to do some more thinking and idea development.

20 Using words precisely

The main reason for using more formal vocabulary is that it is powerful and precise, enabling you to explain even complex ideas accurately. It is, however, all too easy to use a word incorrectly in a 'nearly but not quite right' way.

Examples:

There is a distinct✗ range of ethnic groups in London. (diverse✓)

Pollution from the new factories has exaggerated✗ the problem. (exacerbated✓)

Polio vaccinations in the 1960s had virtually prevented✗ the disease by the 1970s. (eliminated✓/eradicated)

The data infer✗ that lack of sunlight increases risk of depression. (indicate✓)

The UK population is generally✗ 60,000,000. (approximately✓)

Here are some words commonly used across all disciplines; how many of them would you be able to use with confidence in your own writing?

comprehensive (adj.)	differentiate (v.)	phenomenon (n.)
controversy (n.)	explicit (adj.)	prevalence (n.)
correlation (n.)	factor (n.)	quantitative (adj.)
despite (adv.)	fluctuate (v.)	underlying (adj.)
deviation (n.)	implicit (adj.)	

You need to use active learning strategies if you want to develop your word knowledge:

▶ Note down words that you think are useful or that keep cropping up in your reading. If you are not sure which are the most useful words to learn, find books, online guides and dictionaries that give 'common academic vocabulary'.

▶ Look up words in a good dictionary, preferably one that gives the word in example sentences. When you look up a word, take note of the information it gives about grammar and style and, importantly, which other words are commonly used with the key word – there are 'collocation dictionaries' that give this information.

▶ Note that some common words have different meanings in specific subjects or contexts (e.g. *solution*).

▶ You will need to learn subject-specific terms so also use a subject-specific dictionary.

▶ Most importantly, practise using new words in your writing.

Summary

- It's your job to make your assignment easy to read, not the reader's job to work hard to understand what you are trying to say.

- Developing a detailed written plan will save you time and almost definitely result in higher marks.

- Structuring your assignment clearly is essential.

- Each paragraph should have a coherent structure.

- No amount of signpost phrases or formal vocabulary will make up for poor content or confused ideas.

- Even very complex ideas can be conveyed via a simple structure and succinct writing.

- Use words precisely.

- It's better to explain something well in simple language than poorly or incorrectly in complex language.

- Developing your writing style for academic work will take time.

Essential element 5: Rewrite like an expert

21 The process of writing and rewriting

Brilliant assignments are the result of a lot of planning, drafting, rewriting and checking. When you start working on your assignment, you probably won't have a clear position on the title (this is a good thing as you should have an open mind, not a closed one) and you will also be writing more for yourself than for your reader. By the time you reach the stage of a third draft, however, you should have arrived at an informed position and have a reader-focused piece of work.

Stage in the writing process	Development of your position on the issue	Gradual change in audience from you to your reader
1 Understand the point of your assignment title	Your initial thoughts and views on the main issue.	
2 Outline plan based on your initial ideas		Brainstorming, notes on your ideas – **for you**.
3 Reading and research	Development of an informed position through analysis and evaluation of reading.	Notes, summaries and reflections on your reading – **for you**.
4 Detailed plan in paragraphs		Written plan to develop your argument – **for you**.
5 Further reading/research if necessary		
6 Final detailed plan, e.g. 8–10 paragraphs for a 2,000 word essay.	Awareness of gaps or faults in your argument. Possible adjustment of position.	Final plan and first drafts in clear paragraphs – **for you and your reader**.
7 First draft. Check against plan and title.	Development of thoughts, ideas and argument and decision on an end position.	

Stage in the writing process	Development of your position on the issue	Gradual change in audience from you to your reader
8 Second draft. Check against plan and title. Add introduction and conclusion if not done earlier. 9 Third draft. Check against plan and title. 10 Finished final assignment.	Full development of thoughts and position that are explicitly and clearly explained in logical stages.	Development of a clearly structured piece of work – **for your reader**. **For your reader**.

Don't worry about grammatical errors in the early stages but do check for them in your final drafts and use feedback from friends, colleagues and tutors to identify mistakes you typically make. You may only be repeating the same few mistakes but these can build up and detract from your work, so it is worth doing a bit of corrective grammar homework in order to resolve them.

Below is a list of the most common errors students make, with the technical grammatical terms given in brackets for your reference.

Sentence grammar

1 Wrong form of the word (adjective, noun, verb, adverb)

Countries are making changes to suit tourisms ✗ / tourists ✓.

There is still a potentially ✗ / potential ✓ market.

2 Incorrect mix of singular and plural for the subject and verb (subject–verb agreement)

The number of tourists ~~have~~ / has ✓ increased.

Smith et al. (2000) ~~reports~~ / report ✓ that this level of violence is harmful.

Recent research also ~~show~~ / shows ✓ that the drugs are effective.

3 Incorrect switches in verb tense

You can use more than one verb tense in a sentence.

Two UK surveys (Avery 2006, Hallam 2003) have found that the main consumer concern is use of pesticides, but a recent government study reveals a different picture.

However, be careful not to incorrectly mix tenses that should have the same time frame:

The solution was put into the test tube and ~~has been heated~~ / was heated ✓ to …

4 Sentences that are missing a main verb or clause (fragment sentences)

~~Although there are several advantages.~~

Although there are several advantages, there ✓ is also one major drawback.

~~The experiment, which was conducted by a team in London.~~

The experiment, which was conducted by a team in London, will be ✓ published next week.

5 Joined sentences that should be separated (run-on/fused sentences)

These decisions can have significant implications, most managers do not receive adequate training. *Replace the comma with either a semi-colon or full stop.*

The web is a constantly developing technology, this can cause data security problems. *Replace the comma with either a semi-colon or full stop.*

6 Wrong choice of *to + verb* or *verb + ing* after the key word (infinitive or gerund)

The model is capable to make / capable of making accurate predictions.

The failure of cells from removing / to remove sugars causes diabetes.

7 Incorrect sentence structure for direct questions

The issue is if / whether this will lead to an increase in violence.

Research was conducted to see what was the cause of the disease / what the cause of the disease was.

8 Wrong word before or after the key word (preposition, collocation)

I will discuss about violence / discuss violence in computer games.

They are both at / in a constant state of balance.

9 Incorrect use of *the* (definite article)

There are some groups among the ~~society~~ / among society ✓ that object to this research.

The study shows that immune ~~system~~ / that the immune system ✓ is extremely complex.

Punctuation

10 Using commas with *that*

Just about the only time you use a comma with *that* is in the phrase *that is*.

My meeting is on the fourth, that ✓ is, Tuesday.

It has been shown in this essay that, this ~~is~~ not the case.

It is illogical, ~~that~~ people think pollution is not important.

11 Incorrect use of commas with *which/who* (relative clauses)

If the *which/who* part of your sentence is **essential information**, do not use commas:

Authors who ✓ disagree with Carr are Esty and Collins.

If the *which/who* part of your sentence is **additional information**, do use commas to separate this information from the main clause:

Svennson and Wood, who disagree with Carr, propose a dynamic model of business ethics.

Business ethics, which has become increasingly important, can be defined as principles of behaviour as applied to business organisations.

12 Incorrect use of apostrophes

The apostrophe is never used to indicate a plural, and in formal writing you shouldn't really use short forms (e.g. *do not > don't, it is > it's*) so only use apostrophes to show possession:

The scientific community *of this country* > *this country's* scientific community

The article *of Dr Ashi* > *Dr Ashi's* article

If a proper noun ends with an *s* you can follow the normal rule and write *s's* or drop the second *s*:

The theory of *Dr Jones* > *Dr Jones's theory* or *Dr Jones'* theory

Also note that personal pronouns (*his / hers / its / ours / yours / theirs*) do **not** use an apostrophe:

The title is 'Expression' > Its title is 'Expression'

The controversy over global warming stems from the uncertainty of it's / its main cause

Other common areas of error are incorrect use of:

▶ linking words such as *however/nevertheless/whereas*
▶ word forms in a listing sentence e.g. (parallel structures)
▶ capital letters
▶ commonly confused words – e.g. *such as / namely, there / their / they're, affect / effect*.

Do some homework on these if you have problems with them.

What went wrong here?

This second draft of a paragraph still needs some improvements and corrections in structure, vocabulary and grammar. Corrections are given on the right, but you might like to cover them up and have a go at redrafting the paragraph yourself first.

Draft paragraph

The present financial crisis is a product of worldwide globalization. It can be submitted that the financial crisis results in an increase in the need for litigation, an increase in litigation means financial gain for the law firms. During which the world's have experienced a boom and bust cycle that no doubt will continue to repeat itself.

Comments

Worldwide is redundant — globalization is by definition worldwide. Also, the 'topic' sentence has no relevance to the main point of the paragraph, so delete

An overly formal and inappropriate phrase for an essay (comes from a phrase used in court)

This is a run-on sentence — needs more than a comma

Sentence is irrelevant, is a fragment sentence, and uses an empty persuader (no doubt)

A review compiled by Anne Lee Gibson, a top American Lawyer who specializes in competition law showed that the top Am Law 100 firms total revenue increased by the greatest percent in each of the three years preceding the appearance of the three recessions since 1984.[6] Recession results of debt, however debt can be valuable when a company goes bankrupt as many have in recent recession, lots of trading debts occurs, this can result in major profit as it is the lawyers who arrange the trading.

Irrelevant information

firms should be firms'

What does 'increased by the greatest percent' mean? percent should be percentage

Run-on sentences — should be split into two or three separate sentences

Wrong preposition: in not of

Wrong subject—verb agreement. Debts is plural so the verb form should be occur (no s)

You can't just say major profit — should be a significant profit or perhaps large profits

Top tips for rewriting and editing

- Read and redraft your work at least three times.
- Leave at least an hour between each revision – half a day or overnight is even better.
- To help you to see what you have actually written rather than what you think you have written:
  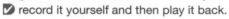 use printouts for checking drafts rather than checking them on screen
  ✔ read your work aloud
  ✔ get someone else to read it out to you
  ✔ record it yourself and then play it back.

First draft

Ignore language/minor mistakes and check the draft against your plan:

☐ What are your draft's overall strengths and weaknesses?

☐ Does the argument make sense?

☐ Does it answer the assignment title?

☐ Are there any gaps or irrelevancies, e.g. background information, description, digressions?

☐ Should anything be in a different order?

You might need to do additional research, fill in gaps, fix flaws in your argument, cut out irrelevant sections, adjust your final position, and rewrite whole sections.

Second draft

All of the above + the following:

☐ Do your introduction and conclusion match up?

☐ Does your conclusion *really* answer the assignment title, the full title and only the title?

Check *each* paragraph in the body:

☐ Is the content directly relevant to the assignment title?

☐ Which sentences give the topic, explore it and say what the point of the paragraph is?

☐ Are any paragraphs too long or too short?

☐ Is *your* voice shining through as the dominant one?

Third draft

Read it aloud:

☐ Does the flow/structure need improving or clarifying?

☐ Does each paragraph follow on clearly and logically?

☐ Where do you need to be more brief, authentic, precise and powerful?

☐ Read each sentence aloud – will each one be clear to the reader? Is each sentence grammatically correct as a whole?

☐ Have you given a reference or reminder phrase every time you use a source?

Fourth draft

Where could you still be more brief, authentic, precise and powerful?

☐ Read each sentence aloud again – check again for grammatical, punctuation and spelling errors.

Final check

☐ Check again that you have given some type of reference every time you have used a source.

☐ Check that you have followed the assignment instructions for presentation, reference list/bibliography and any other work (e.g. notes) you are required to submit.

Summary

▶ Making mistakes and changes is a positive part of the writing process.

▶ Concentrate on content, general flow and style and don't worry too much about minor grammatical errors until your third draft.

▶ You will probably get *much* higher marks if you go through your assignment at least three times.

▶ Learning to read your work with an outsider's eye will enable you to judge the clarity and correctness of your writing.

▶ Being able to edit your own written work is a valuable career skill, and clear written communication is one of the top five employability attributes.

Final comments

Your tutors give you writing tasks to see whether you have understood the point of the question and whether you have engaged with it at a deep level. Thinking develops writing and writing develops thinking, so don't think of your assignment as separate from studying your subject.

Care about what you write and develop a sense of ownership – it's your name on the cover sheet. Your interpretation of the title, your choice and evaluation of sources, and the conclusions you come to are what make your work unique.

Analyse and take action on the oral and written feedback you get on your work so that your next assignment is even better than your last one. As you progress through your course, think also about how the knowledge and issues you discuss in different assignments connect and relate to each other – not just within one module but also between modules and between levels of study.

You should also gradually develop an awareness of where authors and researchers currently position themselves in your subject – where and how brightly do their stars shine in the disciplinary galaxy? Writing is an important way of identifying where your own star is currently positioned in this galaxy, of joining in the discussion of your discipline and of becoming part of your academic community.

Useful sources

Copus J (2009) *Brilliant writing tips for students*. Basingstoke: Palgrave Macmillan.

Godfrey J (2013) *How to use your reading in your essays* (2nd edn). Basingstoke: Palgrave Macmillan.

Godwin J (2014) *Planning your essay* (2nd edn). Basingstoke: Palgrave Macmillan.

Pears R and Shields G (2016) *Cite them right: The essential guide to referencing and plagiarism* (10th edn). Basingstoke: Palgrave Macmillan.

Williams K (2009) *Referencing and understanding plagiarism*. London: Palgrave.

Williams K (2014) *Getting critical* (2nd edn). Basingstoke: Palgrave Macmillan.

Index

assignment titles,
    analysing, 12–14
    content words, 12–14
    function words, 12–14
    scope, 12–14
    top tips, 11
    understanding, 10–14
assignment types in different disciplines 8–9
    highly valued aspects, 8–9

clear communication, examples 4–5
critical writing 19–24
    analysis, 22
    argument, 23
    common errors in, 25–29
    evaluation, 23
    over generalising, 29
    thinking and writing, 24

editing, *see* rewriting and editing
essay extracts, 4–6, 85–86

final comments, 115–116
five essential elements of academic writing,
    15–16

myths about academic writing, 1–3

non-critical writing, 21–22
    description, 21
    explanation, 22

paraphrase, 40–48 *see also* sources
purpose and context of your writing, 7–9

quotation, 32–39 *see also* sources

referencing, 54–64
    accidental plagiarism, avoiding, 59–64
    emphasising different aspects of source,
        55–56
    styles, 54–55
    'What went wrong here?' exercise, 57
rewriting and editing, 3, 99–101
    checklist, 111–113

editing, common language errors, 102–107
   direct questions, 104
   fragment sentences, 103
   infinitive or gerund, 104
   punctuation, 105–107
      apostrophes, 106–107
      commas, 105–106
         with *that,* 105
         with *which/who,* 105–106
   run-on sentences, 104
   subject–verb agreement, 103
   the, 105
   verb tense, 103
   word form, 102
   stages in the rewriting process, 100–101
   top tips, 11
   'What's gone wrong here?' exercise,
      108–109

sources, use in writing, 31–64
   changes from original text, 45–48
   paraphrase, 40–48
   quotations, 32–39
   summarising, 42–44, 48
   things to watch out for, 48
   'What went wrong here?' exercise, 38–39

summary points at the end of each section
   essential elements of academic writing, 17
   let your own voice shine through, 78
   rewrite like an expert, 114
   use your sources, 64
   write critically, 30
   write for your reader, 98

using words precisely, 96–98

'What went wrong here?' exercises and/or
     examples of poor writing
   draft paragraph, 108–109
   using quotations, 38–39
   using reference techniques, 57
   using reporting verbs and phrases, 52–53
what your tutor wants, 10
write for your reader, 79–98
   abstract nouns, overuse, 92
   authenticity, 95
   brevity, 90
   clichés and phrases to not use, 88–89
   form and formality, 88–89
   noun phrases, 90–91
   passive form, 92
   power, 90–91

precise use of words, 96–98
sentence length, 93
signposting language, 82–83
structure, overall, 80–81
structure, paragraph, 84–86
style, 87–95
succinctness, 94
writing, good example of, 4–6
written voice, own, 65–78
main points, 65
phrases for showing certainty and caution,
    75–77
reporting verbs, 68–69
showing your sources support your point,
    66
using 'I', 3, 71–72
using 'we', 73–74